Mariam studied English Literature and Language Communication at Kingston University and supported children in improving their English skills at a secondary school. Her short stories are inspired through childish perspectives and good morals aided by her faith and beliefs. She wishes to seek and promote more representation of race, cultures and ethnicities in her books to reflect the multicultural society we live in. The simplistic and repetitive style of her books encourage creativity, innovation and originality within children and through this, she seeks to support children to digest information at face value but also absorb the message embedded subconsciously through repetition, imagination and play.

We Are All Special

Mariam James

AUSTIN MACAULEY PUBLISHERS™
London * Cambridge * New York * Sharjah

Copyright © Mariam James (2018)

The right of **Mariam James** to be identified as author of this work has been asserted by her in accordance with section 77 and 78 of the Copyright, Designs and Patents Act 1988.

All rights reserved. No part of this publication may be reproduced, stored in a retrieval system, or transmitted in any form or by any means, electronic, mechanical, photocopying, recording, or otherwise, without the prior permission of the publishers.

Any person who commits any unauthorised act in relation to this publication may be liable to criminal prosecution and civil claims for damages.

A CIP catalogue record for this title is available from the British Library.

ISBN 9781528911375 (Paperback)
ISBN 9781528911382 (Hardback)
ISBN 9781528911399 (E-Book)
www.austinmacauley.com

First Published (2018)
Austin Macauley Publishers Ltd
25 Canada Square
Canary Wharf
London
E14 5LQ

I would like to dedicate this book to my friends and family who supported me and believed in my vision. I especially want to dedicate this book to my son, who was the inspiration behind this text.

I would like to acknowledge Desiri Okobia, who inspired me and gave me guidance to achieve my dream as an author. Ethelbert Metzger, for my outstanding illustrations, you truly are gifted. Lastly, Hannah Bunhu, who shares the same vision to promote ethnic minorities within children's books. May you be inspired and persevere no matter what.

The wrinkle on my nose and
the coarseness of my hair

The colour of my eyes and
the shade of my skin

That's what makes me special.

The croak in my voice and the rhythm in my feet

The love I have for music and dancing

That's what makes me special.

The way I look at the world
and the joy I have each day

I know that I'm not perfect but that's what makes me special!

What makes you special?